Buckland Abbey
Devon

THE NATIONAL TRUST

A home for heroes

Water has determined much of Buckland's long history. Cistercian monks chose this isolated site, in the valley of the River Tavy, because it was close to running water. Yet despite its remoteness, Buckland is only nine miles from the sea, and its later owners included two of the most famous seamen of the great Elizabethan age of sail – Richard Grenville and Francis Drake.

The Cistercian abbey

Buckland was established as a monastic foundation in 1278, the last of 78 medieval Cistercian abbeys to be built in England and Wales. The founder was Amicia, Countess of Devon, who endowed the abbey with vast estates. The cavernous Great Barn is a potent surviving reminder of Cistercian productiveness.

For over 250 years, the monks prospered. However, the austere Cistercian rule gradually relaxed and the attraction of their way of life waned. At the Dissolution of the Monasteries in 1536–40, only the abbot and twelve monks remained to be exiled from the abbey.

Grenville and Drake

In 1541 Henry VIII sold Buckland to Sir Richard Grenville, who, with his son Roger, began converting the abbey into a comfortable house. In 1545 Roger was drowned while

The south front reveals Buckland's origins as a Cistercian abbey

Sir Richard Grenville

Sir Francis Drake

commanding the warship *Mary Rose*, when she capsized off Portsmouth, leaving a son, another *Richard Grenville*, to inherit Buckland and complete the conversion in 1576.

Richard was an ambitious soldier with designs for colonising the New World, but he never secured royal patronage for his schemes. Royal favour was, however, bestowed on *Sir Francis Drake*, who in 1577–80 became the first Englishman to sail round the world. Disillusioned, Grenville sold the abbey to Drake, but achieved immortality by his death in 1591, when his ship, the *Revenge*, was overwhelmed in a heroic stand against a Spanish fleet.

The Drake family

Sir Francis Drake acquired Buckland in 1580. He lived here only fifteen years, but for the next 370 his descendants retained possession – save for a brief period during the Civil War, when the Parliamentarian Drakes were ousted by their old rivals, the Royalist Grenvilles.

Gradually, Buckland was modified to suit the family's changing needs. In the early 19th century, it was remodelled by the architect Samuel Pepys Cockerell, and the agricultural buildings were modernised by the pioneer agronomist William Marshall. Buckland was rented out for much of the 19th century, until in 1870 it passed to Sir Francis Fuller-Eliott-Drake. His daughter Elizabeth lived on quietly at Buckland with her husband, Lord Seaton, until 1937, during which period she restored the Chapel. A year later, disaster struck when the abbey caught fire. It was restored, not entirely sympathetically, during the Second World War and sold in 1946 to a local landowner, Captain Rodd, who presented the property to the National Trust.

Buckland today

Since 1951 the Trust has opened Buckland to visitors with the help of the City of Plymouth, which uses the abbey to display part of its collections. In 1988, the abbey was refurbished to mark the 400th anniversary of the defeat of the Spanish Armada. In recent years, the displays have been refreshed and the Elizabethan garden revived. New features are being added all the time.

The Approach

In 1988 a new entrance was made for visitors, with a car-park linked to the property by a footpath. During its construction, archaeological investigations revealed traces of building and medieval pottery, perhaps indicating the site of a monastic gatehouse. To the right, but not open to visitors, is the Home Farm.

At the end of the path, a flight of steps leads down into the first of several enclosures which were reorganised first by William Marshall in the 1790s and again in the 20th century. This was probably a milking yard, as the early 20th-century stone building ahead served as a cow shed until conversion into school rooms in 1989. Squeezed inside today is a model of the *Golden Hind*, made for the 1953 Coronation pageant in Birmingham. The lavatory block to the right was built as a stable in the early 20th century.

The 'Guest-house'

Although this building is called the Monks' Guest-house, it seems likely that its original purpose was agricultural, designed with stabling below and a hay loft above. It was probably built in the early 14th century with a distinctive stone cornice and a series of granite buttresses intended to support the trusses of the roof. The windows were built as ventilation slits, but most have been enlarged since the 15th century, when conversion into living quarters for the monastery first occurred. It was certainly altered in the 1570s by Sir Richard Grenville, whose arms, with those of his wife's family, St Leger, can be seen above the south windows. The fireplace at the west end of what is now the restaurant also dates from this period. That to the east, which uses cannibalised gate-piers, is probably later.

At the end of the 18th century, Marshall added a cottage on the west end. The smaller single-storey extension to the east end was built in the mid-19th century. In 1919 Lord Seaton turned the Guest-house back into a cattle shed with tethering rings fixed to the south wall. Later a grain silo filled the east end and a grain crusher and hopper were installed to the west.

The Guest-house remained in agricultural use until 1988, when the National Trust restored the building to provide visitor facilities, an appropriate use considering its history. Today the reception area with the kitchens below replaces the silo, the restaurant has taken over the cattle shed, and the shop the grain crusher.

The Great Barn

The Ox Sheds

These are William Marshall's legacy, designed for the ox teams that worked at Buckland until 1881. The sheds were built on a semi-octagonal plan enclosing a dung yard, through which an open rill passed 'for the use of stock'. At the lower end of the yard there is an opening to another former straw yard, enclosed to one side by the east wall of the Great Barn. To the left is the 19th-century Linhay, a traditional Devon building with an open-fronted cattle shed on the ground floor and a tallet (first floor) for fodder above.

'Four aged oxen, or six growing steers, are the usual "plough" of the district …', wrote Marshall, adding, 'they step out with a pace, which a Kentish clown would think a hardship to follow with his high fed horse team.' In 1791 there were 22 oxen on the estate. The sheds were restored for use as craft workshops in 1989.

In 2000 a steel sculpture of an ox, by the Devon artist Jonathan Rodney-Jones, was placed in the yard.

The Great Barn

This is the finest and largest building in Buckland – an indication of the hugely successful farming enterprise pursued by the Cistercian monks. The buttressed walls are about 48m long, 10m wide, 8m high and 1m thick. They are punctuated by 23 broadly splayed ventilation openings, and, high up around the interior, rows of 'putlog' holes, where scaffolding would have been fixed. Above these, the oak roof is arch-braced and secured by wooden pegs. It may have been thatched originally.

Porches project on each side of the barn, both with an upper-floor pigeon loft. When their doors were open, the cross-draught helped in winnowing the threshed corn, which was 'thence flung, from hand to hand to either end of the barn', being too narrow for wagons to turn inside. Marshall recognised the inconvenience of this method and in 1792 made three new doors, which allowed wagons to be driven the length of the building.

The cider press at the north end of the Great Barn dates from the 18th century. By 1844 the estate included 27 acres (11ha) of apple orchard, and the gathered fruit, already pulped in a horse-operated crusher, was pressed beneath the top beam, originally wound down by a wooden screw and subsequently replaced by an iron screw dated 1815. The Buckland farm journals record the consumption in 1795 of 26 butts and one hogshead of cider (nearly 3,000 gallons).

At the beginning of the Hundred Years War in the early 14th century, the monks were granted a licence to crenellate (fortify) as a defence against French attacks. They built a fortified wall linking the barn to other monastic buildings to create a defensive stronghold. Part of this wall remains on the south-east corner of the barn.

In 1941, during another war, the barn was requisitioned as a granary for the Admiralty. It was used for the last time in 1948 to store 1,000 tons of Manitoba wheat.

Tour of the Abbey

The Exterior

Compared to the great Cistercian abbeys of the 12th century like Tintern, Fountains and Rievaulx, Buckland Abbey is of modest size – smaller in fact than the Great Barn. It is, nevertheless, a complex building to understand, particularly its original monastic function which has been thoroughly disguised since its conversion into a dwelling during the 16th century and by subsequent alterations, which have removed the other monastic buildings that once adjoined the church.

The external view of the abbey today, save for the renewed windows and the loss of the roughcast regularly applied in the 18th century, is virtually as Cockerell left it. Beyond the precinct wall, however, the turreted building shown in the engraving survives, now known as Tower Cottage (not open to the public). This may have been the abbot's lodgings until it became the abbey stable block, connected to the main building by a tunnel through which a bell system operated. Beyond it was the Cider House, now converted into a private dwelling.

The first reliable representation of the building appears in 1734, when Samuel and Nathaniel Buck engraved a view of the abbey from the north-east. The print shows the north end of the Great Barn and, beyond it, formal walled gardens, the Tudor east wing, the crossing tower, a north transept and linking buildings to the turret tower of the former abbot's lodgings. Since then the gardens have been altered, the windows of the east wing gothicised, and the north transept demolished. Also gone are the ancillary buildings and all vestiges of the cloisters and the chapter house which, on account of the lie of the land, were almost certainly to the north of the church. Demolition probably occurred in the 1800s, when S. P. Cockerell supervised major changes to the fabric.

The Kitchen Wing

Visitors now approach the abbey from the south side. To the east is Grenville's kitchen wing, expanded in the 18th century to accommodate several comfortable panelled rooms on the second and third floors, now converted into flats. The wing still reveals the retaining arches of the chapels that once issued from the east wall of the south transept at ground-floor level. A door at the south end of the wing is distinguished by the carved stone head of a crowned lady set above it. Legend maintains the head is a likeness of the abbey's founder, Amicia, Dowager Countess of Devon.

The Tower

Dominating the building is the crossing tower, unusually massive for a Cistercian abbey (their earliest churches had none), but the present undulating battlements are an 18th-century addition, which were followed by the curious brick flying buttress on the west flank that acts as a chimney flue. Clearly visible on the tower is the crease of the south transept roof above the crossing arch, filled in by Grenville when the transept was removed in order to light his new hall.

The Pseudo-Transept

South-west of the tower is a short projecting wing, known as the pseudo-transept, built by Cockerell in the 1800s to provide a staircase and a new front door to the house. It is the visitor entrance to the abbey.

The Nave

This is now obscured by two mighty magnolia trees. The upper traceried windows are 19th-century replacements. Turn the corner and the nave's full height becomes apparent, still incorporating the signs of earlier medieval openings and vestiges of its roughcast.

The North Front

This reveals few traces of the transept, cloisters or their related buildings that dimly appear in the Buck engraving, and the wall opposite discloses only blocked openings of medieval origin. Instead there are two castellated porches. The smaller dates from the 1800s and has three carved insignia above the door fanlight: the open-hand badge of a baronetcy; the Drake shield bearing stars either side of a wavy line; and an esquire's helmet. The larger porch was previously a smoking room, the external door being a recent introduction.

The East End

This large wing was built by Grenville to absorb the monastic chancel. In the 1800s dormers were added to light the servants' bedrooms, and several windows given Gothic points and simple tracery. The wing is now virtually hidden by additional service rooms and tall yew hedges.

The roofline of the demolished south transept is still clearly visible on the southern side of the Tower

The Interior

The Entrance Hall

The austerity of the rebuilt Buckland following the devastating fire of 1938 is at once apparent. Only fragments of the Tudor house and the earlier Cistercian Abbey survive, but this lack of architectural substance has allowed greater freedom in the abbey's presentation to visitors.

Journeys

The gallery is so named because a film here considers and examines the career and literal journeys of Sir Francis Drake.
The two showcases facing you introduce the legends of Sir Francis Drake and his status as an icon in English history.

A Royal Game. Bronzed plaster by Sir William Reynolds-Stephens (1862–1943). It depicts an imaginary game of chess in which Queen Elizabeth I pits her wits, and ships, against a devious Philip II of Spain. Elizabeth has won the game, just as the English repelled the Armada, leaving Philip holding one of his bishops. The sculpture was the model for an electrotype edition made in 1911 (now in the Tate Gallery, London).

Murals

These were commissioned for the abbey by Lord and Lady Astor as part of the 1951 Festival of Britain celebrations. The artist was Roland Pym (b. 1920), a mural specialist and illustrator. Two of the murals represent the battle with the Armada in July 1588, a third shows the course of Drake's voyage around the world between 1577 and 1580 and the last portrays his ship, *The Golden Hind*.

Glass

After ascending the stairs, visitors should pause at the landing and look back at *the traceried window*. It was reglazed in 1988 with three panels of engraved glass by Simon Whistler (1941–2005). The panels were commissioned by the National Trust as part of the celebrations commemorating the 400th anniversary of the defeat of the Armada.

One of the Drake colours

Treasures

The gallery is the principal room on the first floor, introduced by Grenville in the 1570s as part of the horizontal division of the nave. In the 19th century it was further divided into a bedroom and two dressing rooms, but the room divisions were destroyed by the 1938 fire and never replaced. Today the gallery contains an important collection of Drake relics, documents and paintings. These are more fully explained by the interactive display.

The principal objects are the Drum, used by Drake on his last voyage to the Caribbean in 1595–6, the Silver Gilt Cup, given by Drake to his friend Sir Anthony Rous, and some of the Royal Standards and Colours flown on board *The Golden Hind* and by his regiment of soldiers.

(Left) This engraved-glass view of Buckland was commissioned from Simon Whistler in 1988 to celebrate the 400th anniversary of the defeat of the Spanish Armada

The Drake Chamber

The Drake Chamber

In 1938 the room was damaged by fire, causing the panelling to be removed and refitted, which may account for its present trimmed appearance. The ceiling was also repaired in the 1950s, but unsympathetically, using a massive steel joist to divide it in two.

Since 1951 the room has been presented as a dining room, using oak furniture brought in from elsewhere, but matching a description in 1846 by the visitor Rachel Evans, who wrote, 'The furniture in general was ancient and time worn'. Many of the furnishings and pictures were bequeathed to the National Trust by the antiquarian Dr C. A. Ralegh Radford in 1997.

Pictures

ENGLISH, 19th-century
Buckland Abbey, c.1830
Watercolour
A sketch of the drawing room showing the ladies of the house seated near the south window (the window has since been replaced).

ENGLISH, 16th-century
An unknown Tudor gentleman
The portrait bears a likeness to the young Edward VI.

ENGLISH, 16th-century
Portrait of an unidentified Elizabethan lady

ENGLISH, 16th-century
Portrait of a Tudor gentleman
Said to be Charles Brandon, Duke of Suffolk, who died in 1545. He was a favourite of Henry VIII, whose sister he married.

Circle of MARCUS GHEERAERTS THE YOUNGER (1561–1636)
An unknown Elizabethan lady, said to be Queen Elizabeth I

ENGLISH SCHOOL, 17th-century
Anne Carew
Dated 1606
The daughter of Sir Peter and Lady Carew and wife of Sir Alan Apsley, Lieutenant of the Tower of London.

MARCUS GHEERAERTS THE YOUNGER (1561–1636)
Sir Henry Palmer (d. 1611)
Dated 1586
Palmer was the distinguished commander of the *Antelope* during the Armada campaign and took part in the Battle of Gravelines; he was subsequently Controller of the Navy.

Furniture

A 16th-century Italian oak *cassone* (marriage chest), with a carved front central panel depicting Venus and a Satyr with Cupid, flanked by figures possibly representing the Four Seasons.

A 16th-century French oak clothes press, panelled and carved with grotesque heads.

A 16th-century oak chest, the front carved with the figures of saints carrying their attributes.

A 19th-century oak settle in gothic style, possibly made up from 16th-century pieces.

Five late 17th-century walnut high-backed chairs.

A late 16th-century oak court cupboard.

A late 16th-century oak sideboard.

An early 17th-century oak refectory table.

In 1998 a new ceiling was designed in the Devon tradition by Jane Schofield and hand-modelled *in situ* by Kervaig Associates using lime plaster. The steel joist was artfully disguised and many aspects of the Abbey's history incorporated in the design. Initials of all those involved in the project are discretely recorded in the frieze, and the names of the modellers on the girth straps of the sheep.

Lifetimes

This gallery provides a series of theatrical backdrops to help understand and imagine the lives of the Cistercian and Tudor inhabitants of the abbey. Historic artefacts have been reproduced for visitors to touch and experience. There are special activities for families and children and a computer display on Buckland's architectural evolution.

The gallery extends the full length of the old abbey nave. By the 19th century the west end had been partitioned into bedrooms and the east end, under the tower, converted first into a laundry and later a chapel. According to Lady Drake, the gallery was originally one room, no doubt used as a long gallery by the Tudor inhabitants and referred to as 'The Great Roof' by Cockerell. The 1938 fire seriously damaged the room and it was rebuilt using steel trusses instead of medieval vaulting, of which only some stone springers survive.

Drake statue

This is a larger than life-size plaster statue of Sir Francis Drake by the sculptor Sir Joseph Edgar Boehm (1834–90). It is a studio model, from the original moulds from which the bronze statues now at Tavistock and Plymouth Hoe were cast in 1883 and 1884 respectively. For many years this statue was exposed to the elements on Haldon Hill, south of Exeter, until brought here and restored by the National Trust in 2002.

Drake coats of arms

Apart from the bones of the vault, the only remaining architectural feature of importance is the granite fireplace within the north crossing arch, with its plastered overmantel bearing the Drake coat of arms. On the left side of the overmantel is a second coat of arms and the date 1655 above the initials RN. The arms belong to the Drakes, but the owner of the initials remains a mystery. On the opposite side are two more shields, one apparently depicting a swimming drake, possibly the arms of the Maddock family, and the other the arms of Gregory, a reference to Elizabeth Gregory, wife of Sir Francis's brother Thomas.

The Georgian Staircase

The staircase rises through four floors with three turned balusters for each tread. On the way down it passes a small medieval spiral staircase (now blocked after a few steps), which originally led into the roof space of the church. A gate near the bottom was installed to keep dogs from the upper floors.

The top landing led to the servants' quarters and a curious raised floor. Traditionally this was known as the tailor's bench, although whether it was used for that purpose is uncertain.

The staircase rising to the left (not open to visitors) leads to the tower room, which by 1832 had been converted into a pigeon house. The door beneath it may be that of the 'closet understair' mentioned in an 1834 inventory. Its contents shed some light on the unseen housekeeping labours in 19th-century Buckland. In addition to a brazure (*sic*), a perambulator and a bedwarmer, there was a variety of specialised cleaning brushes for carpets, furniture, banisters, sweeping, scrubbing and black leading, besides a turk's head brush, two mops, a bucket and a dustpan.

Looking back at the door to the Lifetimes Gallery, you can see a trio of medieval openings above it. Before the 18th-century additions, these would have looked out over the lower chancel roof.

Sir Francis Henry Drake, 5th Baronet, installed this magnificent staircase in the late 18th century.

Pictures

At top of stairs:

After JOHN ROBINSON (active 1715–45)
John Carteret, 2nd Earl Granville (1690–1763)
Lord Granville is shown wearing his Garter robes. He held office as Secretary of State and Lord President of the Council.

Woolwork pictures

The staircase is hung with a collection of wool-work pictures of 19th-century sailing ships. Traditionally, these pictures were made by sailors on long sea voyages.

(Right) The Georgian Staircase

The Georgian Dining Room

This chaste 18th-century room is very different from the dark panelled interiors of its Tudor predecessors. It was fitted out by Sir Francis Henry Drake, 5th Baronet, in the 1770s. Panelling was reduced to a simple dado and the doors surmounted by a convex moulding. On the reverse of a board to the left of the fireplace, the only Tudor feature left, is a red pencilled inscription, *Mr Thomas Rowe 19th April 1772, Master of this Job and Foreman of the Sawyers*. Surprisingly, Mr Rowe also tactfully managed to incorporate a reminder of the monastic church: a carved corbel figure of the ox of St Luke in the north-east corner. By 1800, when Cockerell was employed to modernise the house, this room was known as the new eating room. He recorded how it was hung with flock wallpaper, by then beginning to age, and he recommended 'a general new paper with a plainness of character … rather a light colour, but of a clothy warm appearance and the dadoes to be painted somewhat in tone with the paper to be given an appearance of heighth.' The room has been repainted to achieve a similar effect.

In 1834 the room was equipped with twelve mahogany chairs with leather seats, six elbow chairs and, as was often then the practice, four wainscot dining-tables, which could be moved into the centre of the room as required. Most of the present furniture and pictures are on loan.

Pictures

JOHN OPIE, RA (1761–1807)
Anne Bellett
John Bellett junior
Sir Edward Hamilton
John Bellett

Known as 'the Cornish wonder', Opie was a child prodigy who made his fortune in London painting portraits and Rembrandtesque historical subjects.

JAMES NORTHCOTE, RA (1746–1831)
Captain G. Rous
The Rous family came from St Dominick in Cornwall. In the 16th century Sir Anthony Rous had been a friend and executor to Sir Francis Drake. Northcote was a Devon-born painter who had trained under Sir Joshua Reynolds.

JAMES NORTHCOTE, RA (1746–1831)
Rev. Leonard Troughear Holmes
Dated 1776, when Holmes was living in the Isle of Wight.

CHARLES BROOKING (1723?–59)
A Man of War at anchor in Port Mahon Harbour, Minorca
Port Mahon is the main town in Minorca and a fine natural harbour prized for its strategic importance in the 18th century. Brooking was one of the foremost marine artists of his day.

Furnishings

An early 19th-century mahogany six-leaf concertina dining-table on eight gardrooned legs, sometimes known as a naval table.

A set of nine mid-18th-century-style mahogany dining-chairs and a further three, all in the style of Thomas Chippendale.

A mid-18th-century mahogany semicircular card-table with a folding top.

An early 19th-century mahogany bow-front sideboard in the Sheraton style.

A late 18th-century mahogany bow-front sideboard cross-banded in kingwood.

A late 18th-century mahogany and brass-bound wine-cooler.

An early 19th-century mahogany and brass-bound cellaret.

Two silver tea urns hallmarked London, 1778/9.

A set of four silver candlesticks hallmarked London, 1780.

(Left) The Georgian Dining Room
(Right) The carving of the ox of St Luke in a corner of the room is a survival of the medieval abbey

The Georgian Corridor

The corridor is lit by a large south-facing 15th-century-style window. In the south-east corner is a sculpted corbel representing the eagle of the evangelist St John. The corridor display is devoted to life at Buckland in the 18th and 19th centuries. In particular, the display case contains an assortment of personal things, including Lady Fuller-Eliott-Drake's travelling case.

Pictures

Rev. JOHN SWETE (1752–1821)
The Great Barn
Swete was an indefatigable traveller in Devon at the end of the 18th century. He kept a diary, now at the Devon Record Office, which he illustrated with his own watercolours.

JOHN WHITE ABBOTT (1763–1851)
The Great Barn
Watercolour *c.*1800
White Abbott was an Exeter surgeon and amateur painter, particularly a watercolourist of landscapes.

Sculpture

General George Augustus Eliott, Lord Heathfield of Gibraltar (1717–90)
Bronzed plaster, 1801
Lord Heathfield was a distinguished soldier who made his name by successfully defending Gibraltar against siege by the Spanish between 1779 and 1783. Next to it hangs an engraving of Lord Heathfield's portrait by Sir Joshua Reynolds, which is in the National Gallery. Heathfield's son married Anne Drake, sister of the last Drake baronet.

The Kitchen

The monastic kitchen would have been sited an inconvenient distance from Grenville's newly converted Great Hall and so a new kitchen was built within the angle of the south transept and chancel, allowing easy access to the screens passage.

In 1846 Rachel Evans, an early Buckland tourist, wrote about the kitchen: 'an epicure might have been charmed by the numerous stores arranged around to prepare the costly viandes for his table.' By then the dining room had moved upstairs, and Cockerell had converted a series of smaller rooms near the kitchen for the housekeeper and butler, and provided others each with a special purpose: china and glass rooms, boot room, butler's pantry, scullery, dairy and store room, besides burrowing into the ground to the east to create cellars. A small room is still used for storing wood and faggots once necessary for keeping all the fires alight.

Hearths

The room is dominated by two open hearths. That to the south (far end) is earlier, with a massive granite lintel constructed beneath a relieving arch. Above it are eight pairs of brackets for spit rods and a hoisting wheel, possibly used for turning the spit, but more likely for lifting sides of bacon and ham on to hooks ranged along the ceiling brackets.

The later, west hearth has two built-in bread ovens, but during the 18th century it became outmoded and was blocked up, to be replaced by a row of brick charcoal stoves, a French invention known as stewing stoves. In 1950 the old hearth was revealed during investigations into a damp patch that had appeared on this inside wall.

According to tradition, the antlers above the south hearth came from a stag that once chased Sir Francis Drake up a tree.

Contents

The kitchen is provided with utensils of various dates, many of them of traditional design which changed little over the years. They have all been brought to Buckland from elsewhere, but the 1834 inventory mentions many similar items, notably the spits and the large centre table.

(Right) The Kitchen

The Great Hall

The Great Hall is positioned within the original crossing area of the church, directly beneath the tower and adjacent to the south transept that was demolished by Grenville to bring light to this, the most lavishly remodelled room in his conversion. Its chief glory is the decorative plasterwork of the ceiling and frieze, and an overmantel incorporating the Roman numerals MCCCCCLXXVI (1576), an early date for plasterwork of this quality in Devon.

In the mid-19th century, the hall was equipped with a billiard-table, but later photographs show it hung with family portraits, furnished with a grand piano and the most precious heirlooms from the estate of the great Sir Francis, including his sword and shield above the screen and his drum and banners against the window wall. Today the room is furnished in a 16th-century style.

Plasterwork

The ceiling, with its interlocking ribs, floral ornament and two pendants, was restored after the fire, but the rest survived as Grenville's legacy. At the west end an allegorical scene symbolises his retirement from a military career to the cloistered surroundings of Buckland. In the pastoral scene a knight rests under a vine, weapons piled and his horse tethered. His shield and a skull hang from the tree of life. Bordering the shields on the overmantel are four figures representing the four cardinal virtues. They are: *Justice holding the scales*, *Temperance diluting wine with water*, *Fortitude entwined by a snake* and *Prudence holding a book* [the Scriptures]. Above them, three shield-bearing satyrs conceal the ceiling trusses. The frieze on the east wall includes an elaborate strapwork cartouche supporting three hanging shields.

(Right) The Great Hall

(Far right) Shield-bearing satyrs support the ceiling of the Great Hall

Panelling and screen

Three walls of the room are oak-panelled between fluted pilasters. All around the room an inlaid frieze of holly and boxwood is divided up by carved animal masks and figures in various attitudes, including a musician and sheila-na-gigs (fertility figures). Behind the panelling are traces of stone columns from the old church.

Fireplace

The broad granite fireplace with upturned centre and a herringbone pattern of slate at the back is typical of the 16th century.

Floor

This was laid with pink and white triangular patterned tiles, perhaps imported from Holland. Their level is some 46cm above the floor of the Cistercian abbey, beneath which remain the graves of monks who were buried in the nave.

Furniture

This chiefly comprises 16th- and 17th-century oak pieces. Exceptions are:

A 19th-century oak armchair with an arcaded back, copied from an older version in the Bodleian Library, Oxford, said to be made from timbers of *The Golden Hind*.

Two 16th-century Venetian sweet-chestnut chairs with painted and gilded decoration.

The Chapel

The restoration of the Chapel in 1917 on the site of the abbey's high altar is recorded by a brass plaque on the west wall. Previously, the room had been used as the servants' hall, but when a painted medieval column was accidentally discovered behind the room's 18th-century panelling, Lady Seaton organised a full-scale investigation. A Tudor stone doorway was uncovered, and the floor excavated to a depth of 61cm, revealing fragments of 14th-century glazed tiles portraying, amongst other patterns, a fish and 'a rather nice little dragon'.

The recessed splays of the great east window and windows each side of the altar were revealed, and within the north wall the original aumbry (recess for sacred vessels) was found still in position. Buried in the former fireplace in the south wall were the remains of the piscina (basin), now restored, and enough pieces of a three-bay sedilia (seat) to enable two miniature lierne (ribbed) vaults beneath traceried arches to be rebuilt. Other carved stones, probably from the reredos, were reassembled beneath the altar table. Most tantalising of all were the empty graves at the foot of the altar, including perhaps Amicia's own.

The Chapel was rededicated to St Benedict and the Blessed Virgin Mary, and Lady Seaton's efforts were rewarded when she obtained a licence to celebrate mass (now framed left of the altar), issued by Pope Benedictus XV on 15 November 1917. Further restoration took place in 1987.

Picture

Triptych attributed to Cornelis Engelbrechtsz. (1468–1533)

The Entombment (centre)

The Way to the Cross (left)

The Ascension (right)

Engelbrechtsz was a Flemish artist. The picture was bought by the Rev. Sabine Baring-Gould in 1881 and then he presented it to Lew Trenchard church in north Devon.

Furnishings

A granite holy water stoup (basin). Originally a household mortar, the stoup was set on a reclaimed medieval shaft by Lady Seaton.

Stained glass. Said to be from Rheims Cathedral, rescued from the bombed cathedral by Lord and Lady Seaton after the First World War.

A silver 13th-century altar cross. Originally studded with precious stones, but desecrated, probably at the time of the Dissolution. It was presented to Buckland by Lord Mount Edgcumbe.

The Holy Bible. These two volumes, dated 1717, belonged to the Hole family of Parke, Bovey Tracey, Devon.

The font. Presented by the Rector of Holy Trinity, Exeter, to his church in 1855. The church was deconsecrated in 1968 and the font acquired by the National Trust in 1989.

The Way to the Cross (detail); attributed to Cornelis Engelbrechtsz. (Chapel)

These two little vaults were reconstructed by Lady Seaton as part of her re-creation of the Chapel in the early 20th century

The Virgin of the Annunciation. Nottingham alabaster, 15th-century.

The kneelers. These were made about 2000 by friends of Buckland Abbey. The designs are based on the heraldic achievements of the Drake family and others related to them.

The Chapel Corridor and Exit Lobby

Originally the corridor was part of the abbey choir and later the screens passage linking the Tudor kitchen to the Great Hall. In the 18th century an oak dog gate was added at the stairs end. At the opposite end of the corridor there is a small room, once a chapel off the north transept, which retains the only medieval vault remaining in the abbey. It was used as a smoking room at the beginning of the 20th century but now contains a range of resources for those who wish to learn more about Buckland Abbey and Sir Francis Drake. Both of the computer programmes available in other parts of the abbey can be accessed here.

Picture

EDWIN LONG, RA (1829–91)
Elizabeth Beatrice Drake, later Lady Seaton
(d. 1937)
Lady Seaton was the only child of Sir Francis George Augustus Fuller-Eliott-Drake. She married the Hon. John Reginald Upton Colborne, later 2nd Lord Seaton, in 1887. They succeeded to the abbey in 1915 and immediately began restoring it. This portrait is dated 1884. Long was a portrait painter who later became successful painting large historical and biblical subjects.

The Garden

This is largely a 20th-century creation, which effectively disguises any medieval foundations. The earliest surviving record of a garden is the Buck engraving of 1734 which illustrates the walled enclosures and a circular pond north-east of the abbey. Such formality may have had Tudor origins, but an intriguing reference in a household account book for 1709 refers to a payment to 'ye French Gardener', which may also explain such an ordered plan. Unfortunately, the fate of that garden is unknown and there was no apparent trace of it by the time William Marshall visited in 1791, when he commented only on the encircling gloom of the overgrown land.

Engravings of 19th-century Buckland invariably show the abbey's south-west elevation romantically wreathed in climbers and surrounded by trees, perhaps planted by the 5th Baronet, who was interested in forestry. The effect was judged 'most picturesque' by Rachel Evans in her 1846 guidebook to Tavistock. She was also amazed at the vast size of the trees in the garden. Today the south elevation is dominated by two magnolias, a *M. grandiflora* to the east and *M. delavayi* to the west, probably planted by the Earl of Mount Edgcumbe in 1951. The level lawn north-west of the abbey probably dates from the time of Lord and Lady Seaton in the early 20th century; it was originally used for croquet and now for the occasional game of bowls.

The existing shrubs date only from the 1950s, when a formidable team of advisers to the National Trust, including Vita Sackville-West, made their mark. Their recommendations included the removal of several trees and shrubs then regarded as 'far too Victorian' for Buckland. They were replaced by 'choice shrubs' including eucryphias, camellias, hydrangeas, evergreen azaleas and Japanese acers. The prominent climber *Aristolochia macrophylla* (Dutchman's Pipe) was almost certainly planted at the same date to grow over a large box specimen in the north-west corner.

At a lower level east of the abbey is a small enclosed lawn. It is reputedly the site of the

It is probable that the Herb Garden west of the Great Barn was established after a visit by Vita Sackville-West. The irregular-shaped beds contain over 40 different herbs, including feverfew, comfrey, rosemary, thyme, fennel and Lad's Love, which have been grown for centuries for their medicinal properties.

The garden to the north of the abbey was redesigned in the 1990s in a Tudor style

monks' graveyard, but since it has never been excavated, its true purpose remains a secret. Finally, the garden on the north side of the abbey was redesigned in the 1990s. Originally, an ancient yew avenue bordered its precinct wall, but when the trees were struck down by disease, a garden inspired by Tudor precedent replaced them. It is in three parts. A grassed area at the highest level focuses on a granite monument made up from medieval and 19th-century pieces. Surrounding it are wild flowers that, in season, create a flowery mead. Stone steps descend to a path bordered by a traditional orchard followed by formal beds fenced in by riven treillage (trellis). At its centre is a fountain pool. Radiating out from this are formal knot-garden beds and surrounding the entire area are cobbled drainage gullies and herbaceous borders. The plants are a mix of old-fashioned favourites such as roses, pinks, clematis and peonies.

Sculpture

SOPHIE RYDER (b. 1963)
Three sheep
Galvanised wire
These sculptures are a reminder of the sheep farmed by the monks and their successors at Buckland for over 700 years.

The Cistercian foundation

The Cistercian Abbey of St Mary and St Benedict at Buckland was founded in 1278. It lies on the edge of Dartmoor, hidden deep in the wooded valley of the River Tavy, beside a small and unnamed tributary stream. The Cistercians were very sensitive to the beauty of their surroundings, and the site has all the peace and seclusion associated with the ruins of monasteries of this Order, such as Fountains Abbey in Yorkshire. However, there were always practical reasons for their choice of site – the availability of running water, timber for construction and good building stone in the locality. Buckland offered the immediate isolation 'far from the haunts of men', as decreed by the Order, and the natural advantages essential for a Cistercian settlement.

The origins of the Order

Buckland was a late and very well-endowed foundation, owning from the outset 20,000 acres (about 8,000ha), besides a large outlying estate in east Devon. The community had, therefore, no experience of the poverty and hardships that beset the early Cistercian houses in England and characterised the beginnings of the Order itself.

It originated in France in 1098, when a group of monks retired to the marshy desolation of Cîteaux in Burgundy, from which the Order took its name. Their aim was to renew their monastic vocation by living according to the basic principle of the early 6th-century Rule of St Benedict, the founder of the Benedictine Order. The fervour and self-denial with which they silently followed the Benedictine pattern of worship, prayer and meditation, and the emphasis they placed on the manual work it enjoined, became the hallmarks of the Cistercian Order. On the altar were a cross of painted wood and an iron candlestick, the meagre diet contained neither meat nor grease, and underwear and combs were forbidden luxuries. St Bernard, abbot of Clairvaux from 1115 to 1153, was the driving force behind the rapid expansion of the Order. In 1128, the 'White Monks', so-called because their habits were made of undyed sheep's wool, established the first Cistercian house in England at Waverley in Surrey. Early in the next decade, abbeys at Tintern in Monmouthshire and Rievaulx and Fountains in Yorkshire were founded. Between 1135 and 1154, during the years of civil war in the reign of Stephen, over

40 more came into being.

The Cistercians were warmly received in England by Henry I as a civilising force, pioneers in monastic reform and agricultural practice, eager to settle in remote districts and ready to farm any tracts of poor or uncultivated land donated to them. Unsuitable sites, inadequate endowments and natural disasters drove some of the first generation of Cistercian communities almost to ruin, but they survived to become a major influence in the religious and economic life of medieval England. Buckland remained, however, one of the more obscure houses of an Order which developed, in effect, into a multinational corporation. It represents the final phase of the Cistercian colonisation of England, the last of the Devon foundations and the most westerly in the country.

Founding Buckland

Buckland's founder was Amicia de Redvers, the widow of Baldwin de Redvers, 6th Earl of Devon and Lord of the Isle of Wight. His direct family line became extinct with the death by poisoning of their son in 1262, and her decision to found a Cistercian abbey situated among the de Redvers possessions in Devon was therefore an act of pious remembrance as well as religious patronage. Amicia's daughter, Isabella de Fortibus, already a powerful landowner in her

The 'Buckland Book', an early 14th-century manuscript volume now in the British Library, may well have been used by abbots of Quarr on their visitations to give fatherly counsel and, if necessary, censure. An abbot on his three-day visitation would inquire into the spiritual health of his daughter house, asking about such matters as the observation of silence, and assess the material prosperity of the monastery. At the end, he would request the monks to remember in their prayers their brethren of Quarr. A list of feasts ordained by the Chapter General at Cîteaux is included, giving the day of the foundation of Buckland as 20 April.

(Left) *A reconstruction of how Buckland Abbey might have looked shortly after it was built in the late 13th century*

(Right) *The carving over the entrance door may represent Buckland's founder, Amicia de Redvers*

Buckland Abbey seen from the north. The Great Barn stands out prominently to the left

own right as the widow of the Earl of Albemarle, inherited the family estates and granted her mother land in Devon for the new monastery. In her charter of 1273, Amicia specified those who would be remembered there – Edward I, his predecessor Henry III, their wives and children, and Amicia's late husband, his family and her own. She added comprehensively all her ancestors and descendants. Monks came from the Cistercian abbey of Quarr on the Isle of Wight at Amicia's request, to pray for the 'health of their souls' and to establish Buckland.

The strength of the Cistercian Order lay in its organisation as a close-knit family of abbeys, each new foundation was in the care of the 'mother' house from which it had been colonised, and was visited annually by the 'father' abbot. Although four Cistercian monasteries already existed in Devon – Buckfast, Forde (now Dorset), Dunkeswell and Newenham – Amicia chose Quarr as the mother house of Buckland, for it had been founded by her husband's ancestor, another Baldwin de Redvers, 1st Earl of Devon, in 1132 as an abbey of the French Order of Savigny, which united with the Cistercian Order in 1147.

By the time Buckland was established, some of the early idealism had been eroded. Much of the primitive austerity of the early Cistercians had been abandoned and regulations relaxed. Withdrawal from the world had proved impossible, and the fame of the Order now rested on economic success rather than on religious zeal. Yet its unity and stability were maintained, a tribute to the vision and ability of St Stephen Harding, Abbot of Cîteaux in 1109–13.

The site of Buckland Abbey is ancient. An Iron Age earthwork lies to the east of the cloister area, and the name Buckland has an Old English derivation, 'book-land', written in a book of Crown leases. When the first abbot, Robert, and his seven monks came from Quarr in 1278, they found a landscape where the main features of Devon were already marked out: high banks, deep lanes and enclosures, some right up to the limit of the cultivable area of the uplands. Towns, parishes, manors and roads are named in Buckland's charters in contrast to earlier monastic charters, which may give only natural features to indicate boundaries.

The rivers Tavy and Walkham formed the western and northern limits, and a third river, the Plym, marked part of the eastern boundary as it flowed south to Plymouth. The stream that finds its way past the abbey down to Lopwell Quay on the Tavy served as the southern boundary. In this settled, populated countryside, Amicia gave the monks the manors of nearby Buckland (known therefore as Buckland Monachorum), Bickleigh, Walkhampton and the more distant, but valuable, Cullompton in east Devon. With these manors came their inhabitants: freemen, villeins and serfs and their families and goods. Moreover, the grants included mills, fisheries, woods, moorland and all the rights and privileges of a manor.

Managing the estate

There is all too little information concerning the management of Buckland's estates. The economic prosperity of the Cistercians owed much to their use of lay brothers, and by integrating them into the life and work of the community the Order made a notable contribution to medieval society. The purpose of a lay brotherhood was to free the 'choir monks' (the term used to differentiate them from the lay brothers) from the more mundane tasks associated with a monastery, but this reserve of unpaid labour tempted the monks to assemble widespread estates. These were consolidated into specialised units, known as granges, usually for sheep farming.

Two circumstances made it difficult for Buckland to establish the traditional Cistercian pattern of estate management. Firstly, the abbey knew the system of a lay brotherhood only when decay was setting in. By the late 13th century it was becoming much less easy to recruit suitable lay brothers; they were drawn from the locality, usually illiterate and often a liability – rebellious, disloyal and too fond of beer. In 1274, while negotiations for the founding of Buckland were in progress, the Chapter General allowed houses with a dearth of lay brothers to employ hired servants in the monastic kitchen. (Hired labour had been permitted from the first, but never before within the cloister.) Secondly, the structure of established, manorial agriculture inherited by Buckland in 1278 did not lend itself to the creation of the ranch type of farming characteristic of Cistercian granges. Nevertheless, there is evidence, both documentary and archaeological, for the presence of lay brothers at Buckland and for estates farmed as granges.

The 14th century was critical for most Cistercian abbeys. Poor harvests, wars against France and Scotland, the Black Death and the consequent economic and social disturbance, and the shortage of lay brothers dictated a

Penned sheep from the early 14th-century Luttrell Psalter (British Library). The Cistercians were skilled sheep-farmers

complete change of policy. In 1335, the Chapter General finally permitted houses with over-stretched resources to lease granges for rent to outside tenants; the monks therefore ceased to be involved in their management, and the lay brotherhood withered away. Successive outbreaks of the Black Death ravaged Devon from 1348, and the 'poverty of the abbey' is referred to in 1356. But recovery in the county as a whole was quick, and records of the leasing-out of granges seem a feature of Buckland's estate administration only in the next century, for instance Walkhampton from 1486. Certainly by the abbacy of Thomas Olyver (1461–1508), Buckland, like other houses of the Order, was no longer concerned with any direct interest in farming its properties, beyond keeping 'in hand' a home farm for immediate monastic needs.

The Cistercians had a genius for sheep farming and wool production. Buckland missed the peak period of this prosperity in the first half of the 13th century, when the Order's wool exports made an important contribution to the national economy. However, wool was certainly produced at Buckland. In 1347, when Edward III demanded financial aid from the greater monasteries in his war against France, the wool crop of Buckland was so valuable that the abbey ranked second in the list of Devon houses to be approached. Oats was the staple crop, rye was grown, rough pasture abounded for livestock, cattle could be pastured free on the fringes of the royal forest of Dartmoor, and cloth had been woven from the rough wool of the native Devon sheep 'time out of mind' in Roborough, according to a 15th-century petition to Parliament. A document of 1356 lists among the other produce of the area: flax, poultry, calves, lambs, geese, doves, piglings, milk, cheese, butter, honey and wax, hay, apples and vegetables.

Building the abbey church

In view of Buckland's late arrival on the Cistercian scene and its extensive endowments, it is all the more surprising that the architecture of the abbey marks a return to the austerity and simplicity of the first foundations of the 12th century. In accordance with Cistercian requirements, Amicia would have had to provide temporary buildings to await the monks' arrival; an oratory, refectory and dormitory were necessary from the outset, 'so that the monks may immediately serve God and live together in religious discipline'. The Buckland community was never large. Only seven monks came with Abbot Robert from Quarr, instead of the apostolic number of twelve normally sent out to colonise a new settlement. In 1539, twelve monks left the abbey at its dissolution.

The construction of an abbey church was begun as soon as possible. It is an impressive unity, all of one build of the late 13th century with no later extension. The cruciform building is small, set 27 degrees north of east, with four bays in the nave and two in the chancel. Traditionally, the church of an abbey was set upon the highest part of the site. At Buckland, by contrast, it lies tucked into the steep slope of the Tavy valley below the uplands of Roborough Common, possibly terraced into the hillside. The stone is a slate, known locally

The abbey tower still dominates the north front

The west front

'dwelling-place and church' of Buckland during the Hundred Years War, when the French threatened Plymouth and the surrounding district.

The west front of the church reveals emphatically the almost archaic nature of Buckland's Cistercian architecture, severe and plain. Traces of the original west windows can be made out, single-light openings and simple mouldings of a very restrained pattern, for the early Cistercians believed that colour, carving and ornament distracted the mind from duty and devotion. The west doorway recalls the days of the lay brothers, who used this entrance into the west end of the nave reserved for their worship. They attended fewer services, but the whole community came together for the three great feasts of the Christian year, Christmas, Easter and Ascension. When the lay brothers were no

as shillet, which has been used for all the abbey buildings, and is found in quarries close to the church. The dressings are of local Roborough granite, a soft type of granite which weathers like limestone. The exterior remains very much in the primitive Cistercian manner, devoid of ornament, a well-proportioned and compact mass of grey stone, totally in harmony with its environment.

The tower above the crossing appears to dominate the abbey in defiance of the early Cistercian prohibition of towers. In the early 16th century, a wealthy abbey like Fountains could afford to raise a fashionable tower in the Perpendicular style, evidence of the change in Cistercian attitudes over 400 years. In England, however, low Norman towers were often built, and at Buckland the effect of height is due mainly to the later removal of the transept roofs. The original roof line of the south transept is clearly visible on the southern face of the tower. Moreover, it is likely that there was a low coping in place of the present battlements, which are not medieval. The crenellations on the north side of the chancel roof belong to the defensive works carried out as a result of Edward III's licence of 1337 to crenellate the

The monks' day

The heart of monastic life was in the abbey church, where the 'opus dei' (the work of God) was performed in the daily round of worship, the seven offices or services of the Cistercian liturgy. A slow form of Gregorian chant was used, and the compiler of the Buckland Book refers to the ignorance and neglect of the old ways too prevalent in monasteries of his Order; his purpose was to revise the musical content of the liturgy and root out any modern accretions. Buckland was in the traditional pattern, both in architecture and liturgy a return to the old purism. The day was divided into worship and work, the latter now interpreted in a much wider sense, but occupying the customary period of four hours morning and afternoon. A third aspect was the 'lectio divina', times of slow, meditative reading to foster spiritual growth. Cistercian abbeys had no schools and only novices were instructed; truth was revealed through spiritual vision, not intellectual attainment. Prayer was the essence of the silent Cistercian vocation.

This traceried arch in the Lifetimes Gallery once formed part of an outside window looking east over the abbey chancel

longer part of the abbey establishment, the first three bays were probably sealed off, and the space may have been assigned to domestic use or storage. The floor was lowered to create a cellar during the 20th century and the opportunity for detailed examination thus destroyed. The last bay of the nave and the crossing where the monks sat became Grenville's Great Hall, entered from the north side. It is almost certain that the nave would have been of vaulted wood.

The structure of the church is best appreciated on the top floor, where a long gallery was made after fire destroyed much of the building in 1938. At the east end of this, one stands high up under the crossing, enclosed within the four transverse arches. On them the stability of the entire building depended, and the stone springers of the vault merit inspection. But the most notable feature is the lower east arch, pierced by an opening filled with Decorated tracery of the 14th century and rebated for glass. This window at one time overlooked the chancel roof, implying that its roof must have been lower than those of the nave and transepts – a further indication that Buckland preserves characteristics of the first Cistercian churches.

Traces of the medieval church can be identified throughout the interior. Typical are the late 13th- or early 14th-century mouldings, akin to those at Netley, the Cistercian abbey in Hampshire: the stone corbels on the first floor, which are carved with the symbols of two of the Evangelists, the winged ox of St Luke and the eagle of St John; and the circular staircase winding up the thickness of the corner of the vanished south transept just inside the visitors' entrance on the left.

The cloisters

The family relationship of the Cistercian monasteries was emphasised by the common layout of their buildings, although allowance was made for local conditions. After the construction of the abbey church, the drainage and plumbing were of primary concern. The Cistercians were the finest water engineers of their age. At Buckland the contours of the site and the drainage made it necessary to place the cloister to the north of the abbey, as at Quarr; in most English houses of the Order, it lies to the south. There are no standing buildings in the cloister, although limited excavation has indicated that substantial foundations remain to be uncovered in the future. To envisage the medieval monastic scene at Buckland, one must therefore turn to better preserved Cistercian cloisters such as that at Fountains Abbey, where the Chapter House, refectory, kitchen and lay brothers' range can be clearly identified.

The area of the cloister at Buckland must have been restricted, since the nave of the abbey church was no more than 24m in length, and this formed the south side of the cloister. Here, in the shelter of the covered alley that protected the monastic cloisters, the monks sat during periods of the 'lectio divina' and heard the evening reading at Collation, facing north through the stone traceried openings. To their right rose the bulk of the north transept of the church. This formed the north end of the east cloister range, seen in the Bucks' engraving of the abbey dated 1734 and demolished probably in the 1800s. The central room in this range was the Chapter House, where a chapter of the Rule of St Benedict was read every morning to the monks when they assembled for the daily Chapter Meeting to deal with the religious and secular business of the community.

Over this range stretched the monks' dormitory, situated so that they could process in their night boots straight into the north transept and down into the choir at about 2.30am, to keep their Vigils, the first service of the day. Their 'reredorter', or latrine block, would have been situated at the far end of the dormitory. Cistercian planning was a model of convenience and efficiency, for it was important to conserve time and energy in an existence devoted to 'the work of God'.

The location of the northern cloister range is marked by a section of medieval wall, opposite the church. This would have contained the refectory, flanked in this case by the warming house to the east and the kitchen to the west, the latter so placed that the monks' refectory could be served through a hatch on one side and the lay brothers' refectory on the other. The north cloister wall contains blocked windows and doorways which, it has been suggested, might be associated with the fireplace or ovens of the kitchen.

The two buildings situated outside the wall, Tower Cottage and the Cider House, which do not belong to the National Trust, are monastic in origin and have been much altered. Tower Cottage may have been the abbot's house, placed, as in abbeys of this Order, in the more secluded area of the monastery near part of the infirmary, where the Buckland community would benefit from a more clinical approach to everything from serious injury to general 'aking'.

Excavation round the Cider House confirmed the presence of medieval buildings which almost certainly represent the north-west corner of the cloister. This would, in typical Cistercian plan, have been associated with accommodation for the use of the lay brothers. Their quarters formed the entire west range of the cloister, giving them direct access to the court outside.

The industrial area of the establishment lay around and behind Tower Cottage and the Cider House, beyond the north cloister wall. There were workshops for the masons, the smiths, the carpenters and the abbey bakehouse and brew-house. Beside the stream were fish-ponds and on the bank quarries and orchards.

The 'Guest-house'

The long, two-storey building on the steep slope above the abbey (now the National Trust's shop and restaurant) was constructed as a stable, which at some time in the late monastic period was converted to domestic use. Although it may then have become a guest-house, it is more probable that it was a dwelling for the reeve or farm manager, in charge of the home farm of the monastery. The roof is of great interest, a 15th-century structure to judge from the large size of the Roman numerals cut in the timbers to guide the carpenters. The last bays at the east and west ends have been added later, and features like the chimneys and fireplaces are also post-medieval. During the last hundred years before the Dissolution of the Monasteries such a building would be well adapted for the needs of a farmer, his cattle and storage, for the wider doorways would have given the access needed by cattle.

The Great Barn

The outstanding architectural feature of Buckland is the Great Barn. It was clearly planned for a prosperous community and belongs to the same period as the abbey church, about 1300. It shows the same reliance on mass and proportion to give an impression of strength and endurance. Its dimensions seem to dwarf the church, and it is set obliquely only 24m from the chancel. The exterior elevations derive their dignity and rhythm from a progression of buttresses, closely spaced and interspersed with narrow slit windows. An arch-braced roof of 15th-century date was constructed over the vast, shadowed interior. The putlog holes where the medieval scaffolding was inserted are still open, and dovecotes remain above the great medieval doorways. The barn would have been used for storage, the crops, wool and hides from the abbey's estates gathered in at each end, and a winnowing area in the centre.

The Dissolution

The transfer of power at the Dissolution of the Monasteries was all too easy. In 1528 Abbot Thomas Whyte was forced to resign by the Marquess of Exeter, who was steward of the abbey and Henry VIII's cousin. He went unwillingly, protesting that despite his age he could still carry out all his duties, although he could not ride. He asked that John Toker, known to be of 'untoward conversation', should not succeed him. Nevertheless, Toker became abbot in 1528 and set about exploiting his position. He leased the tithes of Buckland Monachorum and other churches of the monastery to his brother, Robert, and his two nephews, and Robert was in addition a well-paid bailiff of Cullompton.

Such malpractices were but one symptom of the malaise affecting religious institutions in general in the early 16th century. At his accession in 1509, Henry VIII had seemed the model of an enlightened Renaissance prince, and men like Abbot Huby of Fountains had hoped for the reform of the Church from within the ecclesiastical establishment and the religious foundations. Huby's ambition was to re-establish the primitive Cistercian values through a revival of spiritual discipline and encouragement of university studies, a policy fully in accord with the scholarly and theological character of the Renaissance in Tudor England. But the 'Great Matter of the King's Divorce' drove the Reformation in England into other channels, in which the king's personal, political and financial motives were paramount. Henry was styled 'Head of the Church in England' in 1534 and the abbeys were doomed, less as obsolete outposts of papal power than as the owners of a substantial area of Henry's kingdom and the guardians of accumulated treasures. Buckland survived the fall of the lesser monasteries in 1536 by having an income of over £200 a year, the cut-off point. Its mother house of Quarr, however, was dissolved and two monks came to Buckland. After three years of uncertainty, and even fear, the greater houses 'went down' in a state of voluntary compulsion. In a sweep of dissolution, Buckland surrendered to the royal commissioner William Petre on 28 February 1539; seven other Devon houses were dissolved within the space of eight days.

Abbot Toker was given a pension of £60 per annum and, in 1557, became vicar of Buckland Monachorum; he was there apparently until 1564. His twelve monks received pensions ranging from £5 6s 8d to £3 6s 8d per annum and eight of them were drawing their pensions as late as 1553. The value of Buckland was assessed at £241 17s 9¼d, Tavistock at £902 and Plympton at £912. No inventory of goods appears to survive, but the treasure of a Cistercian house in lead, plate and furnishings was usually worth much less than its estates. Buckland was leased for £23 3s 5d per annum to George Pollard of Kings Nympton in north Devon, probably the brother of Sir Hugh Pollard, the west Devon commissioner.

The spoils were divided among the King's supporters. Sir Richard Grenville of Bideford, whose ancestor of the same name had founded in 1130 the Cistercian abbey of Neath in west Glamorgan, wrote to Thomas Cromwell in 1539 that he 'was glad as any man of the suppression of these orgulous [vain] persons and devoureres of God's word ... takers away of the wealth of this kingdom and spies of the dewffelys [devilish] bishop of Rome.' Two years later, he was rewarded for his loyalty by being granted the right to buy Buckland. For £233 3s 4d he got the former church, the monastery buildings, the home farm and 568 acres (230ha) of land together with the neighbouring woods. With its barns, dovecotes, orchards, gardens and ponds, Buckland was ideally suited to become a gentleman's residence. The two and a half centuries of Cistercian Buckland had come to an end.

(Right) The Great Barn would have been used to store the harvest from the rich Buckland estate

Sir Richard Grenville

The Grenvilles came from the strip of coast between Bideford and Bude on the borders of Devon and Cornwall, a gentry family established in the area at least since the time of Henry II, perhaps even since the Norman Conquest. Their main home was Stowe, just inside Cornwall in the parish of Kilkhampton, but they also owned a town house on the quay in Bideford (both have now vanished). For generations they had done well, in an unspectacular way; but then, according to the historian A. L. Rowse, 'a new and active strain, of immense and passionate energy' entered the family during the 16th century, along with 'a harsh domineering note … betraying signs of overstrain and unbalance'.

Until October 1540 Sir Richard Grenville the elder (our man's grandfather) was Marshal of Calais, then England's last outpost overseas. When relieved of his command, he returned to England, and in May 1541 was rewarded for his services to Henry VIII by being granted the right to buy Buckland. Sir Richard's particular purpose in buying Buckland was apparently to provide an estate for his son and heir, Roger, then in his early twenties, and he called the place Buckland Grenville. It is clear that Roger lived briefly at Buckland, perhaps in one of the monastic outbuildings, for on 28 August 1544 he buried one son, Charles, at nearby Buckland Monachorum.

Fate frustrated old Sir Richard's plans for this son. On 19 July 1545, as Henry VIII's fleet prepared to attack the invading French off Portsmouth, his flagship, the *Mary Rose*, suddenly heeled over and sank, drowning all but about 40 of the 700 men of board. Among the victims was Roger Grenville, the ship's captain.

So young Richard – born in June 1542 – lost his father at the age of three. His mother married again, and her second husband, Thomas Arundell, settled at Clifton, a few miles down the Tamar from Buckland. There Richard grew up, and the undulating, well-wooded country above Plymouth became more of a home to him than his family's traditional haunts on the north coast 50 miles away.

For a few years Buckland itself passed back to his grandfather, and when he died in 1550, he left the place to his wife, Dame Maude, during

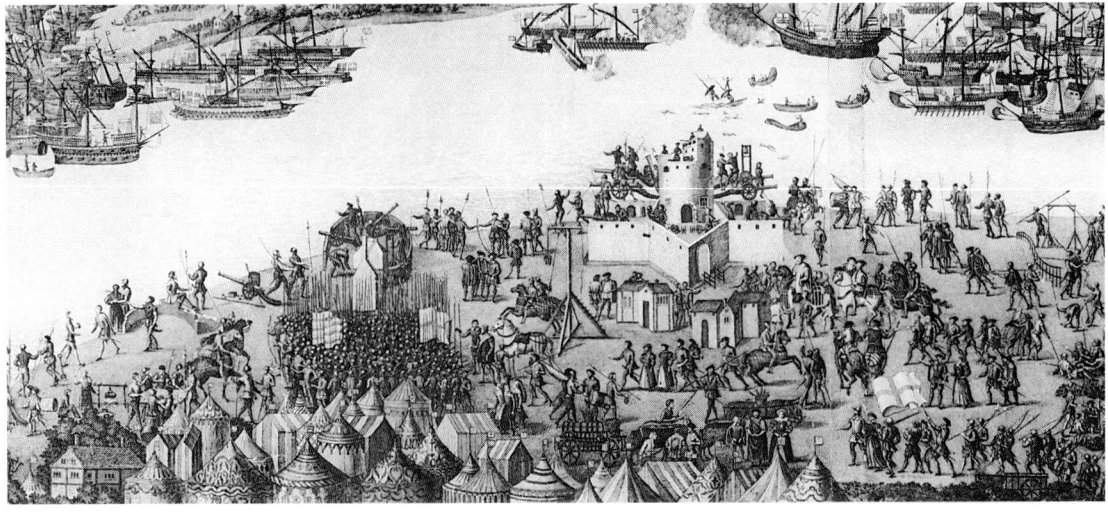

The sinking of Henry VIII's flagship, the Mary Rose. *Among the casualties was the captain, Roger Grenville, Sir Richard's father*

their grandson's minority. She seems to have had plans for turning the church into a house, for old Sir Richard, in his will, specified that she might fell timber for 'the building of the mansion place'. Within a few months, however, she too expired.

The frustrated adventurer

Little is known of Richard's childhood. If he went to school, there is no record of it. More likely he received lessons from a tutor at home. Then, in the autumn of 1559, at the age of seventeen, he went as a student to the Inner Temple in London, which then offered general training in business as well as in law. Not long after his twentieth birthday, on 19 November 1562, the violent streak in his character suddenly erupted, when he became involved in a street fight near St Clement Danes church and ran through Robert Bannester, a London gentleman, with his sword, mortally wounding him – an act for which he may have been briefly gaoled, but for which he was granted a pardon.

On 28 June 1563, soon after he had come of age, he obtained licence to enter his estates. It seems that he was short of money, for he sold some land at Buckland Grenville and Buckland Monachorum, and he did not tackle the remodelling of the abbey, whose church still stood empty. Instead, he returned to live at Stowe, and late in 1564 or early in 1565 married Mary St Leger, the elder daughter of Sir John St Leger, whose home was at Annery, outside Bideford. This generation of the family, also, was cursed with the high infant mortality common in those days: on 10 December the Grenvilles buried their first son – another Roger – in the churchyard at Kilkhampton.

Next, Richard took up the habit of the landed gentry and went off to the wars – in 1566 to Hungary, where he fought under the Emperor Maximilian against the Turks, and three years later to Ireland, where he was appointed Sheriff of Cork and succeeded in putting down a rebellion, but also spent a great deal of money. Again he sold land at Buckland to help finance these expeditions. By early 1570 he was back at Stowe, and a portrait of him

With his fair hair and blue eyes, Grenville is very much a man of Devon; yet it is not the colour of those eyes, so much as the look in them, that arrests attention 400 years later. That steely, challenging glance proclaims Grenville as a man of action, certainly – but also as one harbouring pent-up aggression, who might easily be moved to sudden violence, a dangerous man to cross.

painted in 1571 makes him look every inch the adventurer.

In April 1571 – the year of the portrait – he was returned to Parliament as Knight of the Shire of Cornwall, and thereafter was often in London. Gradually, however, his main interest shifted from land to sea, and in the early 1570s he devoted much time and effort to planning a voyage of exploration in the Pacific and beyond. Fascinated by the challenge and the opportunity, Grenville formed a group of adventurers. Most

Queen Elizabeth, who frustrated Grenville's scheme to sail to the South Seas by her indecision

came from his own family circle, but they included William Hawkins, a merchant of wide experience and by then the leading citizen of Plymouth. Between them, the group could boast four good ships, which cost £5,000 in all; Grenville and Hawkins jointly bought the largest, the *Castle of Comfort*, a powerfully armed private warship of 240 tons. Their hope was that the Queen would take a share in the voyage – which she sometimes did, whether covertly or in the open – and in 1573 Grenville petitioned her to sanction the enterprise.

His first proposal was for a combination of exploration and empire-building: that the fleet should explore the south seas 'for discovery of sundry rich and unknown lands, fatally (and, it seemeth, by God's providence) reserved for England, and for the honour of your Majesty'. The patent he sought was 'to discover lands, territories, islands, dominions, peoples and places unknown'.

The project was presented to the Queen and her Lord Admiral on 22 March 1574, and for a while Grenville thought that royal sanction would be forthcoming. Preparations went ahead. By May his fleet was ready to sail, and the Spanish, getting wind of his plans, denounced him as 'a great pirate'. By June he actually had permission, but the Queen made it contingent on him first giving help to the Earl of Essex, who was beset by difficulties in Ireland. Grenville helped raise a force to fight across the water – and later was commended for rendering such prompt assistance; but by the time the danger in Ireland had subsided, the summer – and the season for sailing – had gone.

Grenville's frustration is easily imagined, and now a sudden change in the political atmosphere conspired to dash his hopes. All through her reign the Queen had been notoriously fickle in her attitude to Spain, vacillating between defiance and co-operation as each course seemed, in turn, the more expedient. In August 1574, after a period of tension, the Convention of Bristol set a new basis for better relations between the two countries; after it the Queen could scarcely sanction an armed expedition into the South Seas, over which Spain claimed a monopoly. So Grenville's licence was withdrawn at the last moment.

Converting Buckland

No doubt it was his plans for a deep-sea voyage that drew him back to live near Plymouth once more. Some time in the early or mid-1570s he at last addressed himself to the task of converting Buckland Abbey into an agreeable home. His scheme for so doing was unusual. He did demolish many of the old domestic buildings and the cloisters; but instead of leaving the

The Grenville arms decorate the windows of the Guest-house

abbey to stand as the village church or go to ruin, and building a new house nearby, as most men did when they acquired monastic property, he converted the church into a dwelling by dividing up the nave into a great hall with two floors of chambers above. He kept the square tower and most of the church's outline intact, but removed the south transept, to let in more light, and built a new service wing with a large kitchen where the visitors' entrance now is, and added a staircase extension. Grenville arms on a window in the building now known as the Guest-house show that he altered that too, although what he did with it is no longer clear.

The result of his labours was a solid and comfortable house rather than a grand one. The building which emerged was certainly unusual, but neither beautiful nor particularly distinguished. Its one grand room, the elegant Great Hall, is modest in comparison with the splendid interiors of contemporary houses such as Burghley in Lincolnshire, yet it contains one feature of compelling interest. Over the fireplace is a plaster frieze showing the figures of Justice, Temperance, Prudence and Fortitude, and above them the date 1576, which suggests that most, if not all, of the rebuilding must have been finished by then.

Grenville settled for the next four years at Buckland, and from that base conducted much business in the West Country, often as a representative of government. In 1577, for instance, as Sheriff and head of the judiciary, he moved against the well-known Catholic recusant Francis Tregian of Golden, near Truro, who had been harbouring a priest, Cuthbert Mayne. Grenville himself led the raid on Tregian's house and took the priest into custody – with the result that Mayne was hung and quartered at Launceston on 30 November, his head being set on a post there, and his quarters on posts at Bodmin, Tregony, Barnstaple and Wadebridge. In the zeal with which Grenville carried out this order from the Council, one can detect at least a powerful sense of duty, perhaps even a touch of officiousness and bloody-mindedness, as if he poured into relatively minor local tasks the energy which he would have liked to expend on larger designs. It is clear that the Government found him a most efficient agent; for his many services he was knighted in October 1577.

Why he left Buckland so soon after completing its reconstruction, we shall probably never know. The reason may have been purely financial: the age was one of inflation, and Grenville perhaps ran short of funds, especially after lending money to his hard-up, hard-drinking in-laws, the St Legers (in return for his taking over their debts, they granted him the fee-simple of the island of Lundy, off the Devon coast). Perhaps, as he reached middle age, he simply wanted to return to Stowe, his family's ancestral home. It may be that he did not much like Buckland anyway. In any event, at the end of 1580 he sold – or, strictly speaking, mortgaged – the abbey to two agents acting on behalf of that master mariner, Francis Drake.

The fine plaster frieze in the Great Hall depicts a soldier who has turned his war-horse loose and sits under a vine, on which he has hung up his shield. Skulls peep from inside the trunks of trees. Does all this signify that Grenville, at the age of 34, had retired from wars and maritime adventure, to live the life of a country gentleman? Given his character and later achievements, that seems impossible. Is the frieze then ironic, the wry comment of a man deeply frustrated by the failure of his attempt to sail the southern ocean and make himself a national figure? Either way, it is a disturbing composition.

Sir Francis Drake

Drake had been born in about 1540 on a farm at Crowndale, a hamlet on the Tavy only three miles north of Buckland, and no distance from Clifton, where Grenville grew up. Yet his background was entirely different. Far from being members of the landed gentry, his family were of yeoman stock, and his father Edmund was a lay-preacher who taught his eleven children at home, largely from the Bible. In 1549, when Francis was only eight or nine, the family was caught up in the violent riots which greeted the New Prayer Book. They sought sanctuary first in Plymouth, then in Kent, where they lived on a hulk in the Thames, and Francis went early to sea on a coaster plying in the Channel. Yet although ships and the sea became his life, he remained at heart a West Countryman and returned to Plymouth or its immediate environs whenever he could. When, at the height of his fame, he chose for his coat of arms the motto *Sic Parvis Magna* – great achievements from small beginnings – the words accurately reflected his rise in the world.

In person, he was stockily built, with round head and reddish beard, a cheerful manner, and

Francis Drake in the early 1580s, at the height of his fame (National Portrait Gallery; on loan to Montacute House)

The Drake coat of arms in the Lifetimes Gallery

the ability to talk straight to anybody, from the Queen down. Enemies called him an arrogant upstart – and no doubt he was; but he was also immensely courageous and energetic, an inspired and inspiring commander of men. At a critical point in his voyage round the world he himself proclaimed to his crews, 'I must have the gentlemen to haul and draw with the mariners, and the mariners with the gentlemen' – and his ability to make all ranks pull together was one of his greatest strengths as a seafarer.

Among the motives that drove him to mighty

deeds, three overriding forces stand out: his burning Protestant faith, his intense patriotism and his hatred of Spain. This last was ignited by an incident on the coast of Mexico in 1568, when, on his first voyage across the Atlantic, Drake had sailed with his cousin, John Hawkins of Plymouth, collecting slaves from the coast of Africa and selling them in the West Indies. All went well until they reached San Juan d'Ulua, the centre of Spanish trade and communications, where the Spaniards tricked and ambushed them. Drake escaped, but was separated from the other ships of the flotilla and returned to Plymouth alone, determined to exact vengeance on Spain.

This he proceeded to do, on every possible occasion, for the rest of his life. Three times in the early 1570s he made successful expeditions to the Spanish Main; on the last, in 1572–3, he captured the town of Nombre de Dios, attacked the treasure trains bringing silver and gold from Peru to the coast, escaped with 300,000 pesos' worth of gold, and returned to England a rich man. Yet of his many marauding voyages, none caused the Spaniards greater chagrin and alarm than his circumnavigation of the globe, achieved between 1570 and 1580.

Sailing round the world

The professed aim of his voyage was closely similar to that of the scheme proposed by Grenville only four years earlier: to explore the south seas, seek new lands in Terra Australis, then make for the Moluccas, and return home via the Strait of Anian. The great difference was that the Queen, who before had denied Grenville permission to sail, now not merely sanctioned Drake's departure, but herself invested in the venture.

Grenville has often been portrayed as a jealous rival of Drake, embittered by his failure to bring off what the other man achieved. There is, however, no evidence to support this view. Drake gained the Queen's backing simply because the fickle political climate had again changed, and whereas a few years earlier Elizabeth had been anxious to pacify King Philip, now she wished to do him active injury, and secretly gave Drake sanction to attack Spanish treasure ships off the coast of Peru.

Drake sailed in July 1577 on board the *Pelican*, with four other ships and a total company of 164 men. By the time he returned to Plymouth in September 1580, he had passed through the Strait of Magellan, sailed up the coast of Peru, ballasted his ship with Spanish silver and gold, landed on the shore of California, crossed the Pacific, reached the East Indies and the Spice Islands, and returned via the Cape of Good Hope, becoming the first English sea captain to encircle the globe.

His achievement, consolidating his earlier reputation, made him by a long way the most famous private citizen in the world. Yet so nervous was he when he returned that he did not dare come ashore until he knew how the political land lay; instead, he anchored in the lee of St Nicholas island, off Plymouth, until his wife and the Mayor came out to meet him. His worries were unnecessary. The Queen summoned him to London, welcomed him in triumph, and, by knighting him on board his own ship (renamed *The Golden Hind*) at Deptford next April, gave open defiance to the King of Spain. So vast was his booty that it was reckoned enough to meet the cost of an entire year's government; most of it was taken under heavy escort to London, but the Queen privately told him to keep £10,000 for himself, and the same for his crew.

While Drake's pockets were burning with Spanish gold, Grenville had again run short of money. So within two months of his return, Drake had agreed to pay the very large sum of £3,400 for Buckland Abbey, its contents and 500 acres (202 ha) of land.

Settling at Buckland

Because Drake did the deal through two intermediaries, John Hele of Plymouth and Christopher Harris of Plymstock, historians believed for years that he tricked Grenville into selling him the estate. But expert analysis of eight contemporary documents shows that Drake's two representatives took Buckland over on a strange form of mortgage, which gave them

Drake's Drum

moved in: perhaps in August 1581, when he gave up the lease of a house which he had been renting in Plymouth; perhaps when he took formal possession of the abbey, in November 1582. The second date seems more likely, for on 17 September 1581 he became Mayor of Plymouth, and during the year of his office had many duties in the town.

Once established at Buckland, he travelled frequently back and forth between there and Plymouth – most often on horseback, sometimes by river. His importance in local affairs stands out from the records surviving in the Widey Court Book, which show how messengers were frequently despatched to him, or ran errands on his behalf: 'Payment to Sir John Humphreys for carriage of letters to Sir Francis Drake ... Sending Sir Francis Drake's warrant to Plympton ... £5 for a supper for the right to hand the place back to Grenville, and to recover their money, if they so decided, in March 1584. In other words, at the end of 1580 Drake *lent* Grenville £3,400; the loan allowed him to inhabit Buckland, and also gave him the unusual right of choosing, after three years, whether to keep the property or hand it back in return for repayment. The implications of the transaction are clear: Grenville urgently needed cash, and Drake was equally keen to invest some of his spoils in property.

Messrs Hele and Harris acted as Drake's attorneys, but he himself must have been directly involved. He surely went, for instance, to inspect the abbey, and so see whether or not he approved of Grenville's conversion. It is not clear when he actually

(Right) Elizabeth Sydenham, painted in 1585, around the time of her marriage to Drake. She is wearing the Drake Jewel (on loan from Plymouth Museums and Art Gallery)

40

The launch of the English fireships against the Armada at Calais on 7 August 1588

Drake and his lady and other justices … Item paid Peter Vosper to go to Buckland to know whether the judges did come.'

Somehow it is hard to imagine this short, square man at ease in his large, square country house. No doubt he entertained handsomely, but one has the impression that terrestrial surroundings meant little to him. His true home was the captain's cabin high on the poop of a ship. Certainly, in the fourteen years during which he owned Buckland, he made practically no mark upon its fabric: apart from some oak panelling, which may possibly date from his time, there is hardly a trace of him – except for a few prized possessions – in the building. It was Grenville, not Drake, who made Buckland what it is.

There is also a certain melancholy in the fact that no children were born to Drake or grew up here. His first wife, Mary Newman, died childless in 1582/3 after thirteen years of marriage; and his second, Elizabeth Sydenham, a beautiful and well-born young woman whom he married about two years later, also failed to produce any offspring. For much of the time, especially when Drake was away at sea, the house must have been empty and echoing.

Just as on the north coast the Grenville family did much to build up the trade and stature of Bideford, so in the south Drake contributed handsomely to the development of Plymouth, promoting the port's trade, improving its defences, and above all directing the construction of a new water supply in the form of a leat, or aqueduct, which ran from the headwaters of the River Meavy at Burrator right into the town.

Yet whenever the Queen needed his services, or would sanction a foray, he sallied forth – to maraud in the Spanish Main in 1585–6, to singe the beard of the King of Spain with his audacious raid on Cadiz in 1587, to play a key role in the Armada campaign a year later, to launch a second (but this time disastrous) raid on Cadiz in 1589, and finally to sail on his last voyage in 1595. For all these grand endeavours, Buckland was his springboard.

During these years Drake's affairs seemed to entwine curiously with those of Sir Richard Grenville. In the mid-1580s Grenville was much occupied with the task of strengthening Cornwall's coastal defences: the curving jetty in Boscastle harbour was rebuilt by him in 1584. But Grenville was also drawn by his cousin Walter Ralegh into projects for planting an English colony in the New World, and in April 1585 he left Plymouth with a fleet of seven ships which deposited 107 men on Roanoke Island, off the coast of Virginia. A year later, knowing that the colonists would need reinforcement and re-supply, Grenville set out again, this time from Bideford – only to find the party gone. And who should have come to their rescue? Drake, who chanced to be passing on his way home, found them in distress and took them off.

Both men fought prominently in the campaign against the Armada – Drake as Vice-Admiral of the English fleet in his flagship, the *Revenge*, Grenville as commander of a flotilla detailed to ferry troops to Waterford and then guard the western approaches against any attempt by Philip's ships to attack Ireland. Again, fate seemed to deal Grenville a poor hand: while he played an efficient but largely negative role in the west, Drake won further renown by capturing the richly laden *Nuestra Señora del Rosario* and her commander, Don Pedro de Valdés, and by harassing the Armada all down the Channel, until the Spanish fleet was dispersed by fireboat attack off Calais and driven headlong up the North Sea.

An immortal death

Grenville, after further service in Ireland, where he struggled to plant English families as colonists in Munster, at last achieved immortality by the manner of his death, in 1591. By then he was a ship's captain of repute: when at sea, he dined, like Drake, off silver plate, to the sound of music, and was said – when in his cups – to crunch up glasses in his teeth until his mouth poured blood. No doubt the stories were exaggerated, but they pointed accurately to his wild temper.

In 1591 he sailed as second-in-command to Lord Thomas Howard, who took a squadron of the Queen's ships, reinforced by private men-of-war, to intercept the returning Spanish treasure fleet off the Azores. Grenville's own command was the *Revenge* – considered by many an unlucky ship, from her habit of running aground and springing leaks.

Off Flores Howard got wind of the approach of a large and powerful Spanish battle fleet, and ordered his squadron to stand out to sea. For whatever reason – whether because half his men were ashore sick, whether because he thought the sails approaching were those of the treasure fleet, or simply because of his own obstinacy – Grenville failed to obey the order, was cut off, surrounded, grappled and boarded by the Spaniards. The crew of the crippled *Revenge* fought off their attackers all day and all night;

The Loss of the Revenge; after Oswald Brierley (National Maritime Museum)

The Burial of Francis Drake; by Thomas Davidson (Plymouth Museums and Art Gallery)

with astonishing courage and pride Grenville refused to surrender until, fatally wounded, he was carried aboard the enemy flagship, where he died a few days later.

The battle has passed into legend as one of the most heroic actions ever fought, immortalised not least by the haunting imagery of Tennyson's poem, and the stricken commander's final words:

I have fought for Queen and Faith like a valiant man and true;
I have only done my duty as a man is bound to do:
With a joyful spirit I Sir Richard Grenville die!

A last expedition

Drake's demise was less glorious. A portrait painted in 1590 shows how much he had aged: his hair had receded, his cheeks and eye-sockets had become hollow, his whole face had sunk. By his late forties even the greatest of Elizabethans had become an old man.

His last expedition to the Caribbean, which sailed from Plymouth in August 1595, seems to have been doomed from the start. His name had lost none of its magic. Men flocked to join him, and a large force was assembled: 27 ships manned by 1,500 sailors, and carrying 1,000 soldiers under Sir Thomas Baskerville. Yet Drake's fellow-commander, Sir John Hawkins, now 63, fell ill during the outward voyage and died just as the fleet sighted San Juan. Then, after unsatisfactory and inconclusive manoeuvres on the coast, Drake himself fell victim to the dysentery which was sweeping through his crews. On 27 January 1596, aboard the *Defiance*, aware that his life was ebbing, he signed his last testament in a shaky hand, leaving his property in England to his younger brother Thomas. As he lay *in extremis,* he was clearly thinking of home, for the document listed his possessions at Buckland, Yarcombe, Sherford and Sampford Spiney.

Next morning, 28 January, Drake died not much over 50 and was buried in a thunder of gunfire within sight of Puerto Bello. 'His body being put into a Coffin of Lead was let down into the sea,' recorded a contemporary, 'the Trumpets in doleful manner echoing out their Lamentations for so great a loss and all the Cannons in the Fleet were discharged according to the Custom of all Sea Funeral Obsequies.'

Drake's heirs

Although none of Sir Francis Drake's heirs ever achieved his national renown, their story over five generations has been meticulously recorded by Elizabeth, Lady Drake, in two volumes published in 1911. She begins with Thomas Drake, the youngest brother and executor of Sir Francis, who succeeded to the estate in 1597 following the death of Sir Francis's widow. Thomas was a sailor, like his brother, who had accompanied him around the world, but on retirement to Buckland he pursued a new career as plaintiff in 'perpetual law suits' against members of his family, neighbours and Sir Francis's debtors. He won most of the actions, but not all were concluded by the time of his death in 1606.

The Drake Baronets

His son and heir was Francis (1588–1637), an Oxford student who, typically for the Drakes, enjoyed an active role in the local community. He became MP for Plympton and later Bere Alston. In 1633 he was appointed High Sheriff of Devon and his support for Charles I was rewarded by a baronetcy. Family matters also concerned him. He extended the estate by buying property at Launceston, Werrington, Yarcombe and Knightshayne, and he enhanced his uncle's reputation by publishing *Sir Francis Drake Revived*, and an account of the circum-navigation in *The World Encompassed*, both books providing important source material on the great man.

At the time of Sir Francis's death in 1637, aged 49, Parliament had been dissolved for eight years and opposition to Charles I was increasing among Parliamentarians, whose leaders included three friends of the Drake family: John Pym, John Hampden and William Strode, father-in-law to Sir Francis. The 2nd Baronet (1617–62), son of the 1st Baronet, and another Sir Francis, had served as a mercenary on the Continent before returning home to marry Dorothea, John Pym's daughter. It was a rash move, for the West Country was overwhelmingly Royalist, including the Grenvilles. After a brief Parliamentary success at the Battle of Modbury near Plymouth, in which Sir Francis took part, fortunes were reversed and Richard 'Skellum' Grenville, the King's general in the west, was rewarded for his military conquests by being granted estates of three Parliamentary leaders: the Earl of Bedford, Lord Robartes of Lanhydrock and Sir Francis Drake.

'Skellum' (slang for scoundrel) determined to exploit the irony that restored his grandfather's house to the family, and he made Buckland Abbey his headquarters whilst he waged a reign of terror on the countryside and besieged

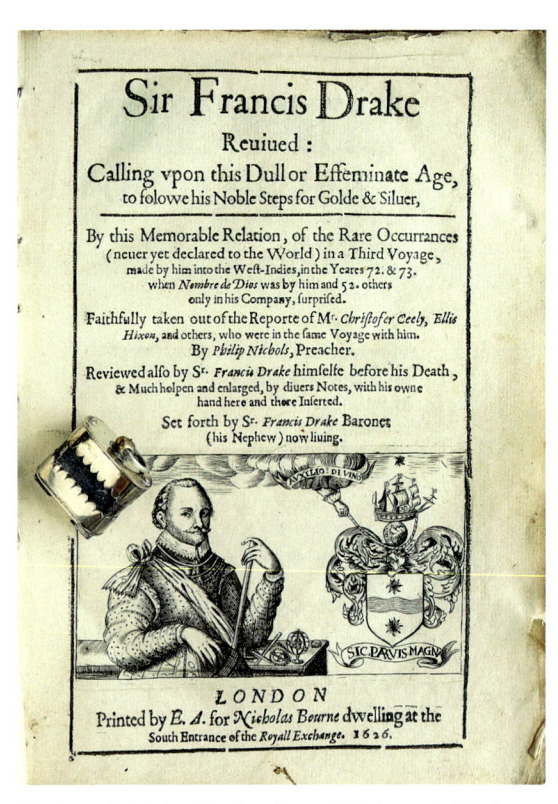

Sir Francis Drake Revived, published in 1626 by his nephew and namesake to keep Drake's memory alive. On it is the Drake lodestone, a magnetic stone used in compasses and said to have belonged to Drake (on loan from Plymouth Museums and Art Gallery)

Plymouth. Sir Francis escaped with his regiment, the Plym Horse, which he himself had raised, and continued the campaign at the Battle of Langport in 1646 and, under General Fairfax, in the Parliamentary advance westward. On 12 January 1646 the general's New Model Army recaptured Buckland and 100 prisoners after a fierce struggle. 'Skellum' had by then retreated to Cornwall and eventually to France, leaving Sir Francis master of his house once more. Fortunately, the abbey did not suffer badly during the occupation. Grenville in fact had built a new riding school in the grounds, but Sir Francis and Lady Drake had suffered from being deprived of their estate and their income, and were forced to petition Parliament for pensions.

At the Restoration the Buckland estate comprised 277 acres (112ha) plus four cider orchards, two gardens, woods, hop yards, nurseries and a small mill. In the abbey itself, Sir Francis is remembered by his coat of arms dated 1655, modelled in plaster above the fireplace in what is now the Lifetimes Gallery. It appears he was a cultivated man, as his library included several Italian classics besides novels and French romances. In 1661 he was pardoned by Charles II for his activities during the Civil War and he celebrated the occasion by purchasing a dinner service for the abbey. A year later, aged only 44, he died childless and was buried in the parish church.

The 3rd Baronet (1647–1718), a nephew, was once again named Francis and was described as having 'a lively genial temperament'. At the age of eighteen he eloped with his cousin, who died young, and he married twice more, amassing thirteen children in the process. He had trained as a lawyer and took an active part in Plymouth affairs as the town's Recorder, but it was as an MP that his legal training proved most useful in that litigious age. In 1679 he supported the Exclusion Bill in favour of the Protestant Succession, thus provoking the Duke of York, the future James II, to bring an action for damages against him in the sum of £10,000. As a precaution against confiscation he conveyed Buckland to friends and relatives until the danger passed. An inventory of the house contents survives and lists a great deal of silver and pewter, two feather beds, 20 tables and cupboards, 48 chairs and stools and five tapestries.

The Georgian dog-gate

Little is known about the 4th Baronet, Sir Francis Henry Drake (1693–1740), described as 'a popular country gentleman'. He continued the family tradition in taking part in local politics, but otherwise lived an unremarkable life. In 1734 Buckland was engraved by Samuel and Nathaniel Buck, the first accurate view of the abbey, still in Tudor guise, bounded to the east by formal gardens and to the north by a cluster of gabled outbuildings. But this ordered prospect and Buckland's destiny was already threatened, because in 1732 Sir Francis had inherited Nutwell Court, Exmouth, in Devon, once the property of his brother-in-law, Henry Pollexfen. As a result, on Sir Francis's death in 1740, his son, yet another Sir Francis, chose to spend more time at Nutwell than Buckland, which a contemporary described: 'this decayed place is a sinker and there is absolutely no forethought in the management', adding, 'it rains into all the rooms of the house', culminating in the collapse of the Dining Room ceiling in 1754.

The 5th Baronet (1723–94) was a stuffy bachelor bibliophile who preferred life at Court, first with the humourless George II, a personal friend, and then George III, following his appointment as Master of the Household in 1771. Perhaps he also avoided Buckland because his mother, the dowager Lady Drake, retained a life interest in the house and allowed a daughter-in-law, wife of Francis's brother Samuel (a distinguished sailor who became a Lord of the Admiralty and Baronet), to use it. Sir Francis's letters suggest he suffered from both melancholia and hypochondria, and he took a dim view of his sister-in-law's attempt to brighten up the old abbey, until in 1768 his mother died and he began to make some improvements. During the 1770s the east wing was modernised by fitting out newly panelled rooms reached by climbing an elegant new staircase, prohibited to dogs by the addition of gates, and the Dining Room was improved with a pine dado. The family seat was once again secured until 1794 when Sir Francis died, childless, like his two brothers who predeceased him.

Buckland revived

A visitor to Buckland at the end of the 18th century was William Marshall, the agricultural reformer, who was researching his book *A Rural Economy of the West of England*. West Devon, he considered, was the most benighted agricultural district in England, with Buckland no exception: 'the situation is naturally recluse, and is now rendered truly so, by long neglect'. Fortunately for Buckland, Sir Francis's sister, Anne, had married George Eliott, son of the dashing Lord Heathfield who had attained fame and fortune by securing Gibraltar against a Spanish siege between 1779 and 1783. Their son, Francis Augustus, had also followed a military career, obtaining the rank of general, and he succeeded both to his father's peerage and his mother's Buckland inheritance.

With characteristic Heathfield energy, Francis Augustus set about restoring Buckland with the help of his architect, Samuel Pepys Cockerell. Cockerell (1753–1827) had a large London practice and now enjoys a reputation for his whimsically oriental-styled Gloucestershire houses of Daylesford and Sezincote. He also remodelled Nutwell Court into an 'exquisitely precise and austere neo-classical mansion'. At Buckland, however, he was restricted, 'to fit up this House merely for an occasional residence', but he was sufficiently aware of its architectural antiquity to write to Lord Heathfield: 'At all Events no alteration must be attempted to the character of the Building.' The same letter makes numerous suggestions for improving the accommodation, but only one recommendation is known for certain to have been carried out – a new staircase at the south-west end of the Great Hall, since rebuilt. A great deal more was undoubtedly done, for, in a second letter from Cockerell to Heathfield dated about 1801, he remarks, 'I find this place in very high order and beauty' before explaining his ideas for decorating some of the principal rooms, and his account to Heathfield at the same period for 'designing and superintending the works at Buckland Abbey' amounts to over £7,000.

William Marshall also worked for Lord Heathfield, not always in harmony with Cockerell, who complained in a letter to his employer: 'I am persuaded that the Agricultural arrangements (as well of the Buildings as the Farming) cannot be better done than by Mr Marshall; but he must excuse me for doubting his knowledge of domestic arrangements of another Character and his taste in decoration.' Despite this criticism, Marshall remained popular with Lord Heathfield, who bequeathed him £450 on his death in 1813, and the extent of Marshall's influence is demonstrated by the surviving farm journals of 1795–1805, which provide a dour summary of endless labour in the fields and barns, six days per week, throughout the year by men, women and children. On average about 20 farm workers, 12 oxen and 6 horses toiled at Buckland with the men earning up to nine shillings per week. Crops included wheat, barley, oats, turnips, potatoes,

The Great Barn; painted about 1800 by John White Abbott (Georgian Corridor)

cabbages, peas, dairy produce, honey and cider. There are separate accounts with specialist tradesmen like the mason, wheelwright, blacksmith, miller, cooper, harness-maker, quarryman and Mr Grear, the mole catcher, who caught an astonishing eight dozen moles in October 1800.

Lord Heathfield died childless, 'having pass'd a life of gentle utility', and Buckland was inherited by his nephew, Sir Thomas Trayton Fuller (1785–1870), a soldier who had fought under Sir John Moore in the Peninsular campaign. He assumed the additional family names of Eliott-Drake and in 1821 was created a baronet, but on retirement to Devon he chose to live mainly at Nutwell Court rather than Buckland, which was advertised to let on 20 July 1815: 'The house is well furnished and fit for immediate reception of a family of distinction'. It comprised three sitting rooms, seven best bedchambers, five dressing rooms, servants' rooms and offices, stabling for twelve horses and three coach-houses. Nineteenth-century tenants included Vice-Admiral Sir Robert Stopford, a Napoleonic war veteran, Sir John St Clair, also a naval officer, and in 1850 Thomas Gill, a Mayor of Plymouth and subsequently the town's MP.

The family return

Sir Thomas died in 1870 and once again Buckland passed to a nephew, Sir Francis George Augustus Fuller-Eliott-Drake (1839–1915). In 1861 he married Elizabeth Douglas, daughter of Sir Robert Douglas of Glenbervie, New Zealand, who in 1911 published her two-volume *The Family and Heirs of Sir Francis Drake,* the scholarly work on which all later accounts have been based. Her interest in her husband's family history extended to Buckland itself, where she and Sir Francis returned to live in 1902 until his death in 1915. Here they maintained a lavishly appointed Edwardian household. 'When the last lady Drake drove from the Abbey to Yelverton, a pair of black horses drew her carriage with two footmen on the box in dark-green uniforms turned out with white.'

Their only surviving child was a daughter, Elizabeth, who married in 1887 the Hon. John Colborne, later Lord Seaton, grandson of Field Marshal Lord Seaton, one of Wellington's generals and a Governor-General in Canada. They repaired the abbey once more, repointing the exterior, following removal of the roughcast applied in the 18th century, renewing the plumbing and above all creating the Chapel on

Elizabeth, Lady Seaton in 1884, wearing the Drake Jewel; painted by Edwin Long (Chapel Lobby; on loan from Plymouth Museums and Art Gallery). She created the Chapel on the site of the abbey high altar

the site of the old high altar. A letter from Lady Seaton states: 'Mr Snell, an architect did a good deal at Buckland Abbey' (H. J. Snell, a well-known Plymouth architect of a number of neo-Renaissance classical municipal buildings .

The Seatons lived quietly. They had no children, and Buckland's valley site surrounded by trees and the old monastic walls helped ensure its isolation. On Lady Seaton's death in 1937 Captain Richard Owen-Tapps-Gervis-Meyrick became the new owner. He was a descendant of the 19th-century Sir Thomas Fuller-Eliott-Drake's brother and the last member of the Drake family to live here, but only briefly. On 6 January 1938 a chimney flue caught fire which spread throughout the nave of the old church. The roof collapsed, causing terrible damage to the building, but the Drake treasures, including the drum, were saved. Repair work began immediately, but although structural restoration was completed within two years, the new fireproof floors and steel-truss roof were more expedient than beautiful.

Two years later, Captain Meyrick sold the west Devon part of the Buckland estate and in 1946 made plans to auction the abbey itself with its neighbouring land. Shortly before the auction, Captain Arthur Rodd, a Yelverton landowner, bought the estate and presented the abbey, its garden, drive and lodge to the National Trust.

The National Trust

At that time the abbey enjoyed neither a collection nor an endowment, but mediation by the Trust with Plymouth City Council solved both problems. In 1951 the Council accepted a full repairing lease of the property from the National Trust (it was renewed in 1970) and converted the abbey into a branch of the City Museum and Art Gallery. The project was financed largely with grant-aid from the Pilgrim Trust, supplemented by the fund-raising efforts of the Friends of Plymouth City Art Gallery and Buckland Abbey, a body which was founded for this specific purpose.

From 1951 to 1987 Buckland was administered by Plymouth as a Drake, Naval and West Country Folk Museum, stocked mainly with exhibits from the museum's collection. By the late 1970s, however, it was realised that the displays needed rejuvenating, and the purchase by the National Trust in 1981 of the remainder of the Buckland estate from Captain Rodd's daughters provided the catalyst for reassessing both the presentation of Buckland Abbey and the relationship between the Trust and Plymouth. As a result, management of the abbey reverted to the National Trust, but with continued financial support from Plymouth, and two new exhibitions in the main galleries were mounted by the museum.

In 1987 the property was closed to allow the abbey to be refurbished and the recently acquired Guest-house to be converted into a centre for visitor facilities. It was reopened by the Countess Mountbatten on 19 July 1988, exactly 400 years after news that the Armada had been sighted off the Lizard had interrupted that legendary game of bowls on Plymouth Hoe. The current exhibitions date from 2003, when the galleries were refurbished.